PANDA
IN THE GARDEN THEMES AND MANDALA DESIGNS

STRESS RELIEF COLORING BOOK

Jupiter Coloring

Printed in U.S.A.

Copyright 2017

All right reserved. This Coloring books or any potion thereof many not be reproduced or used in any manner whatsoever without the exoress written permission of the publisher except.

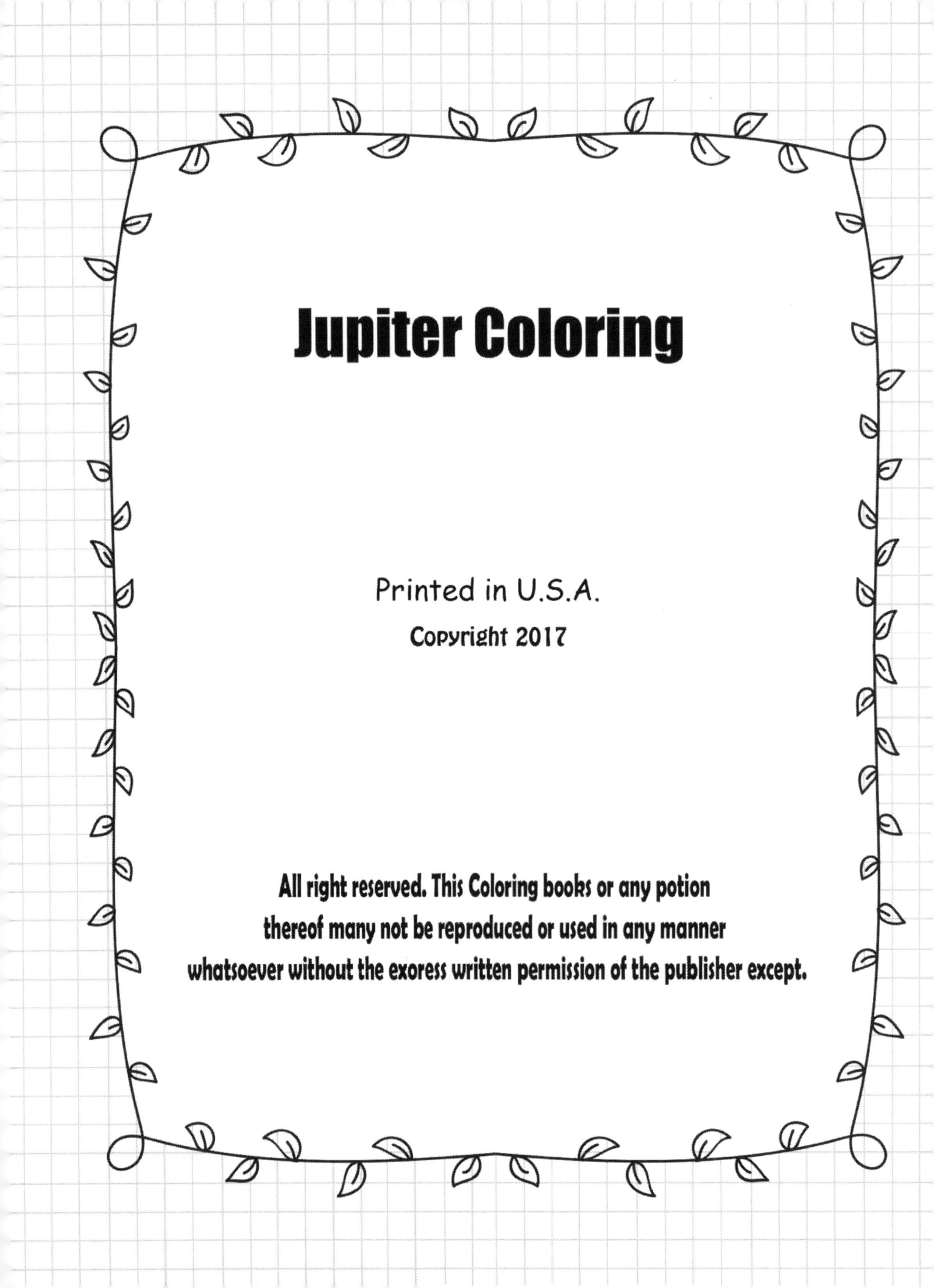

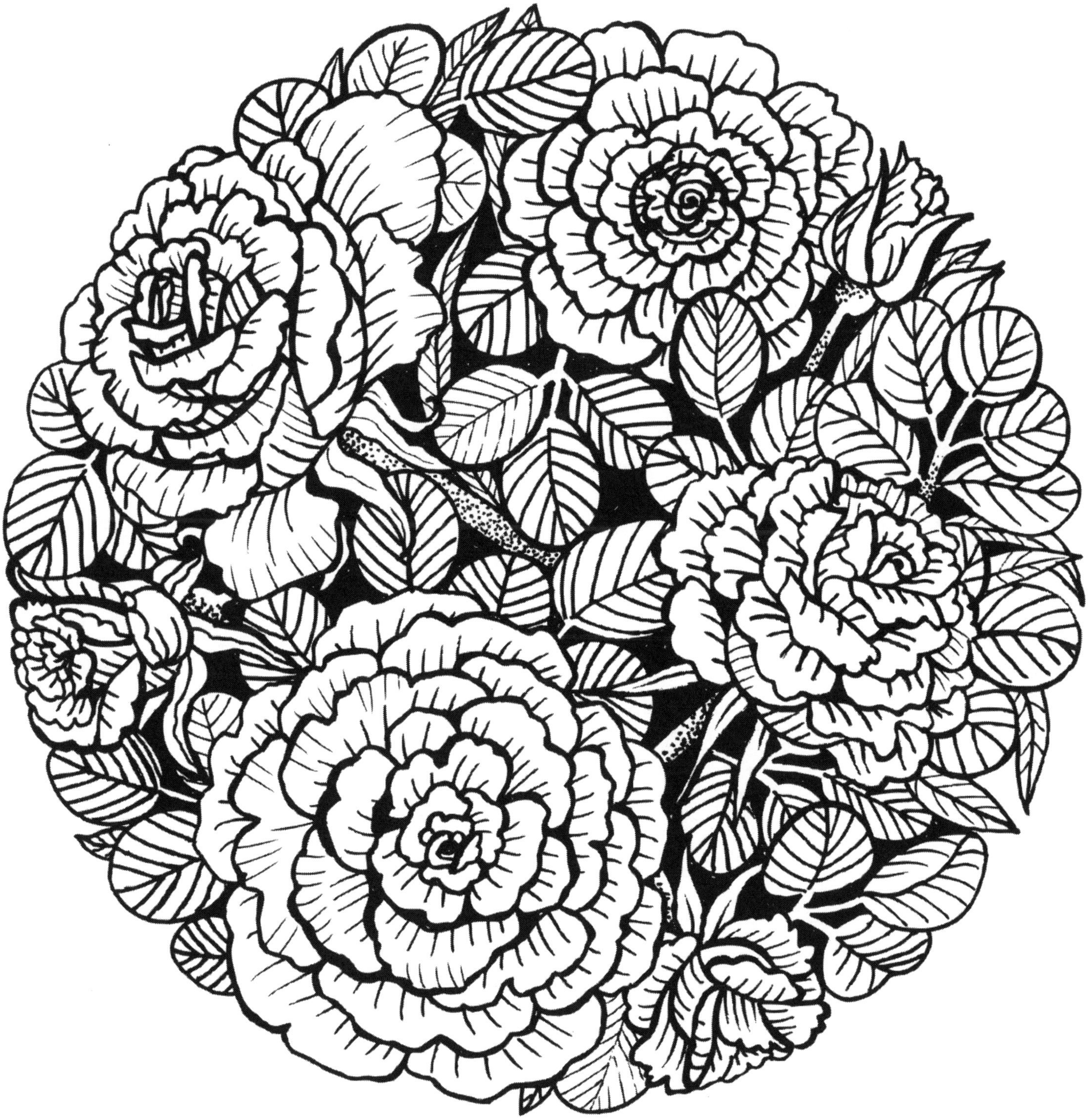

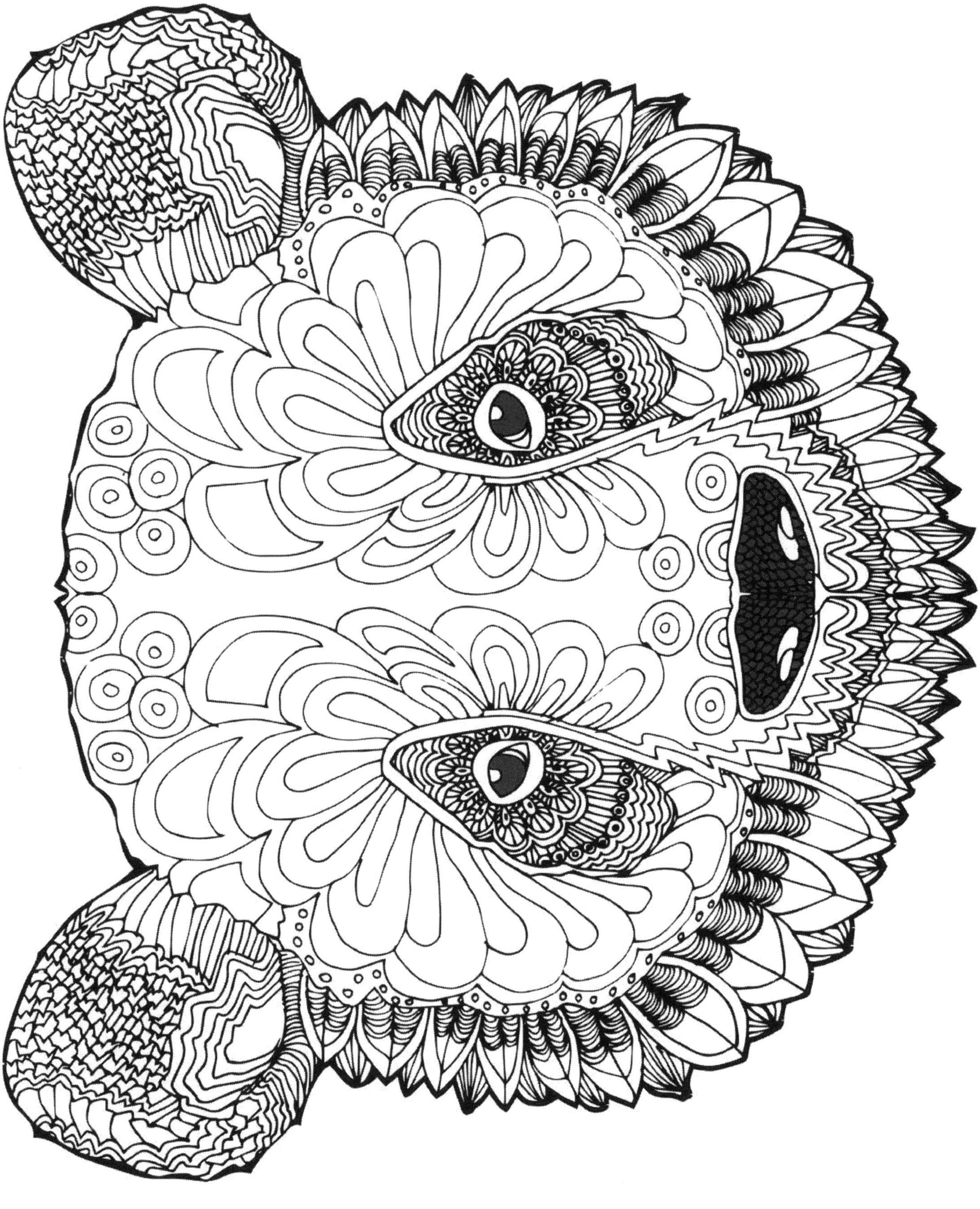

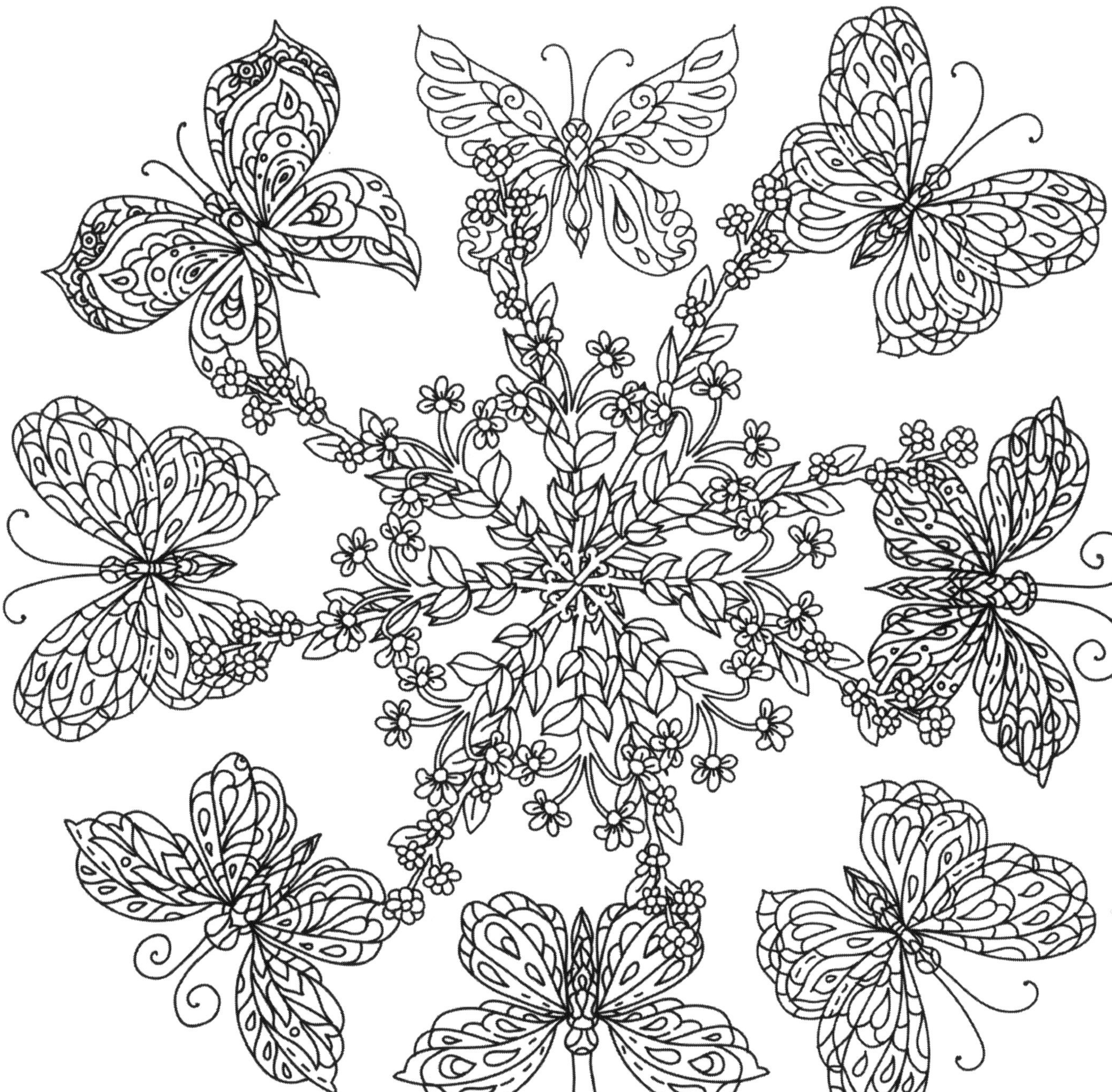

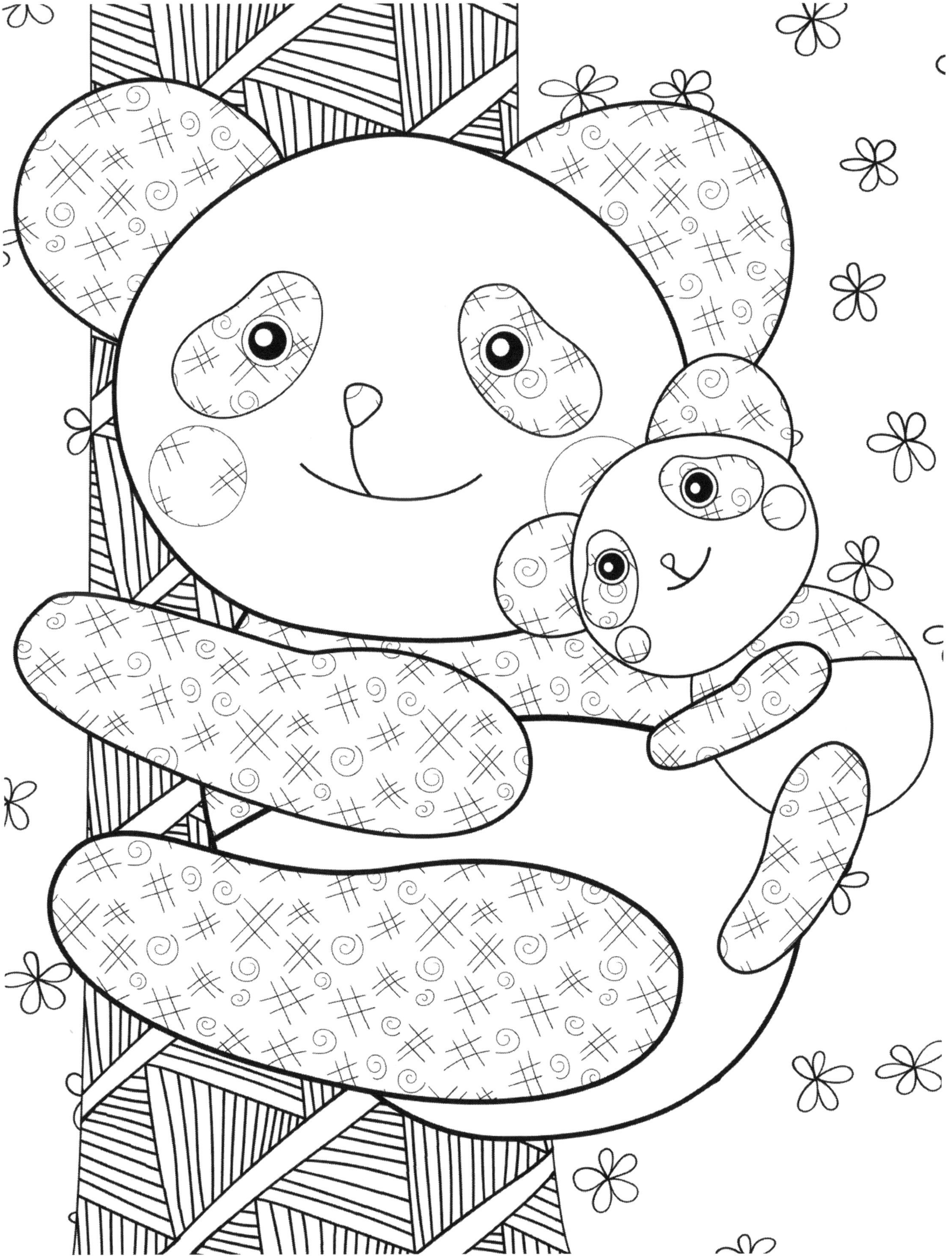

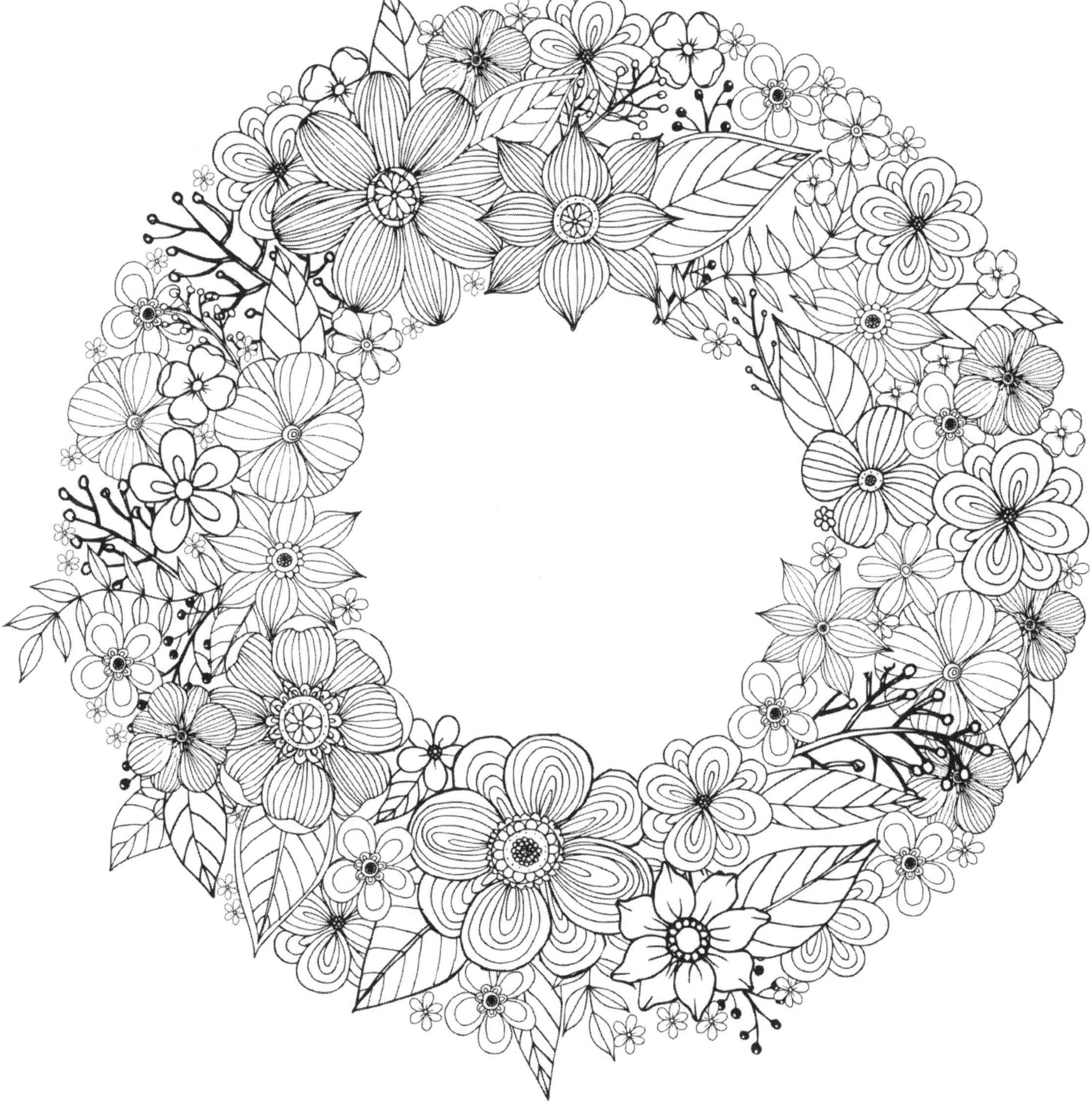

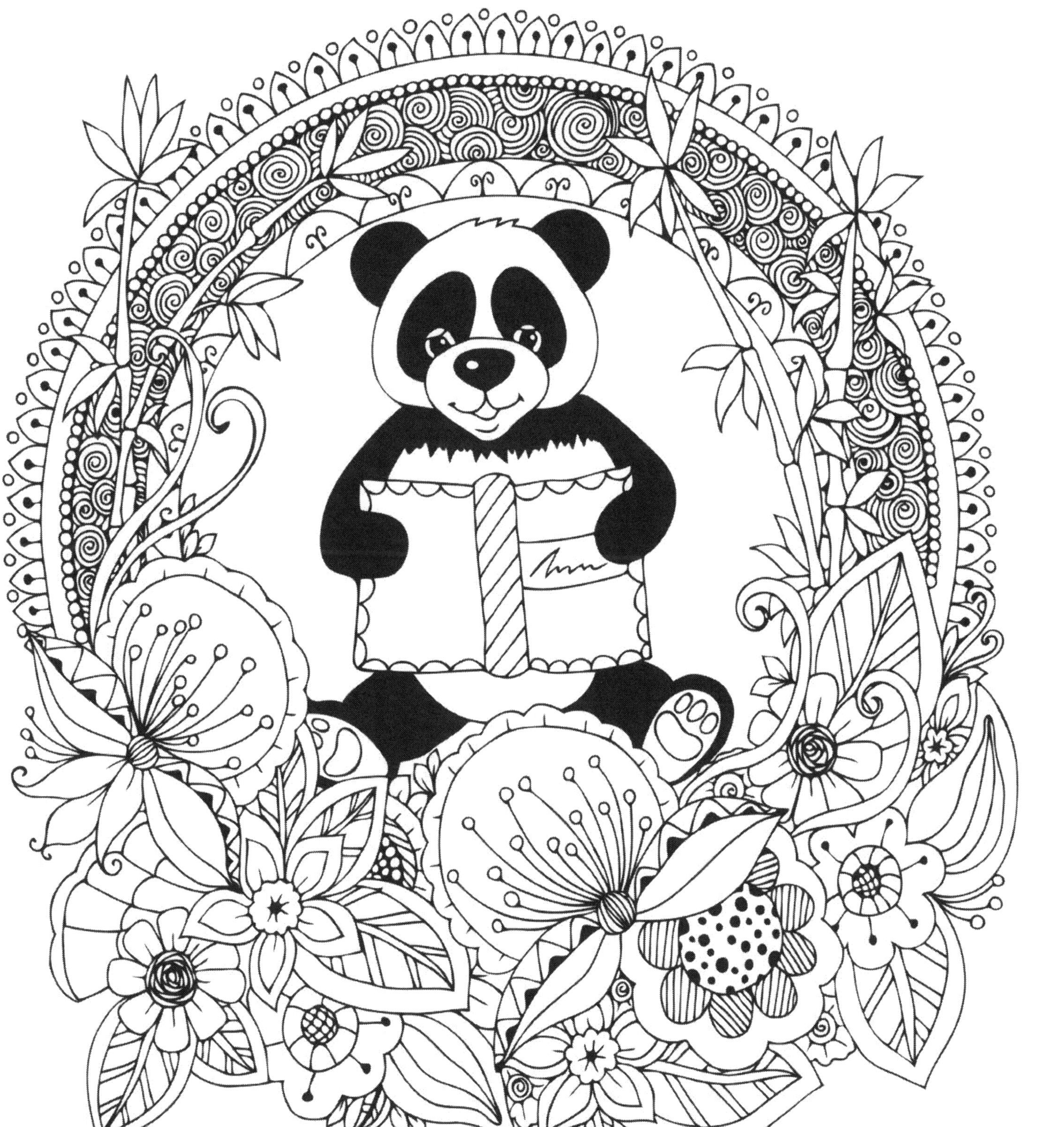

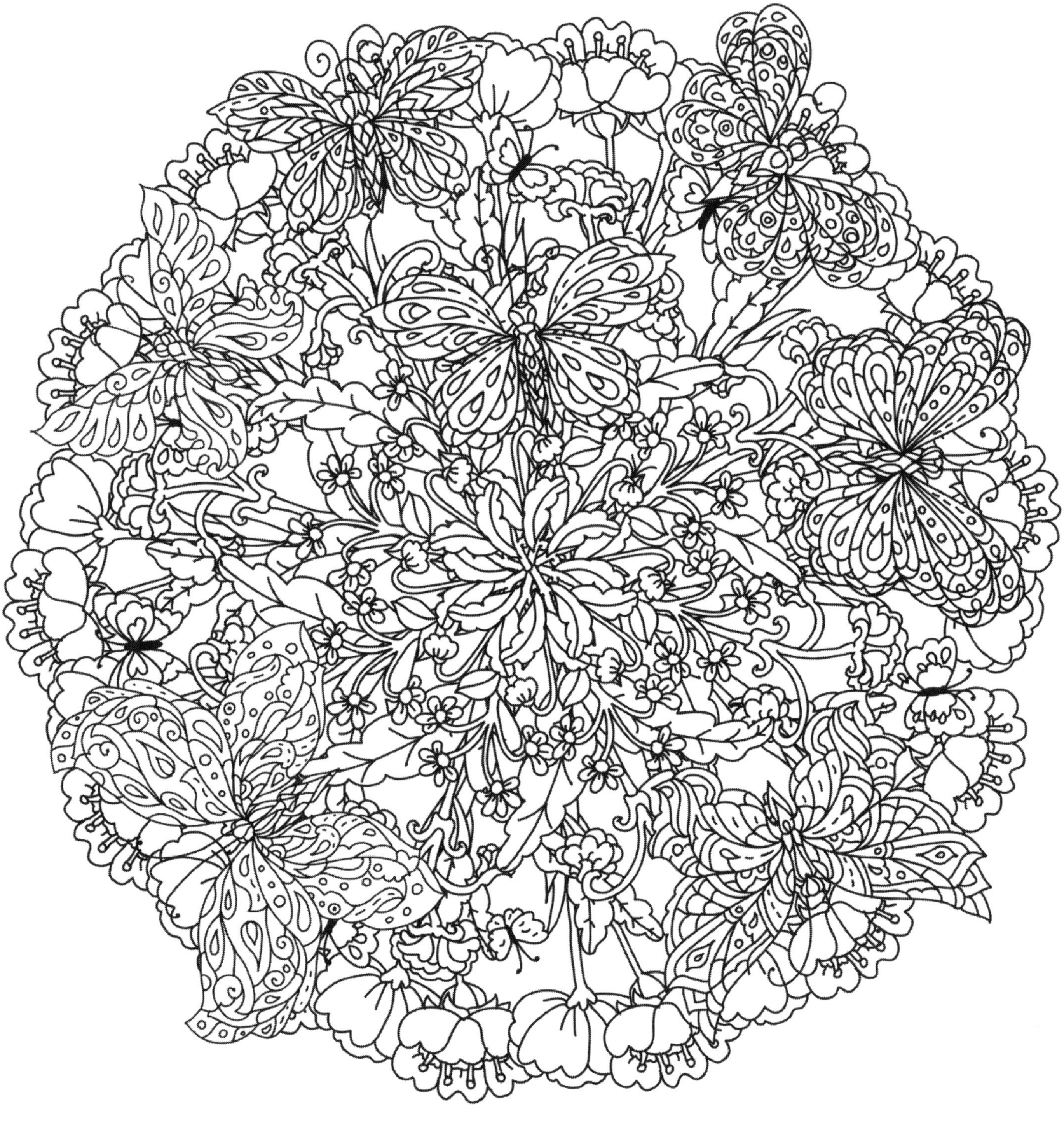

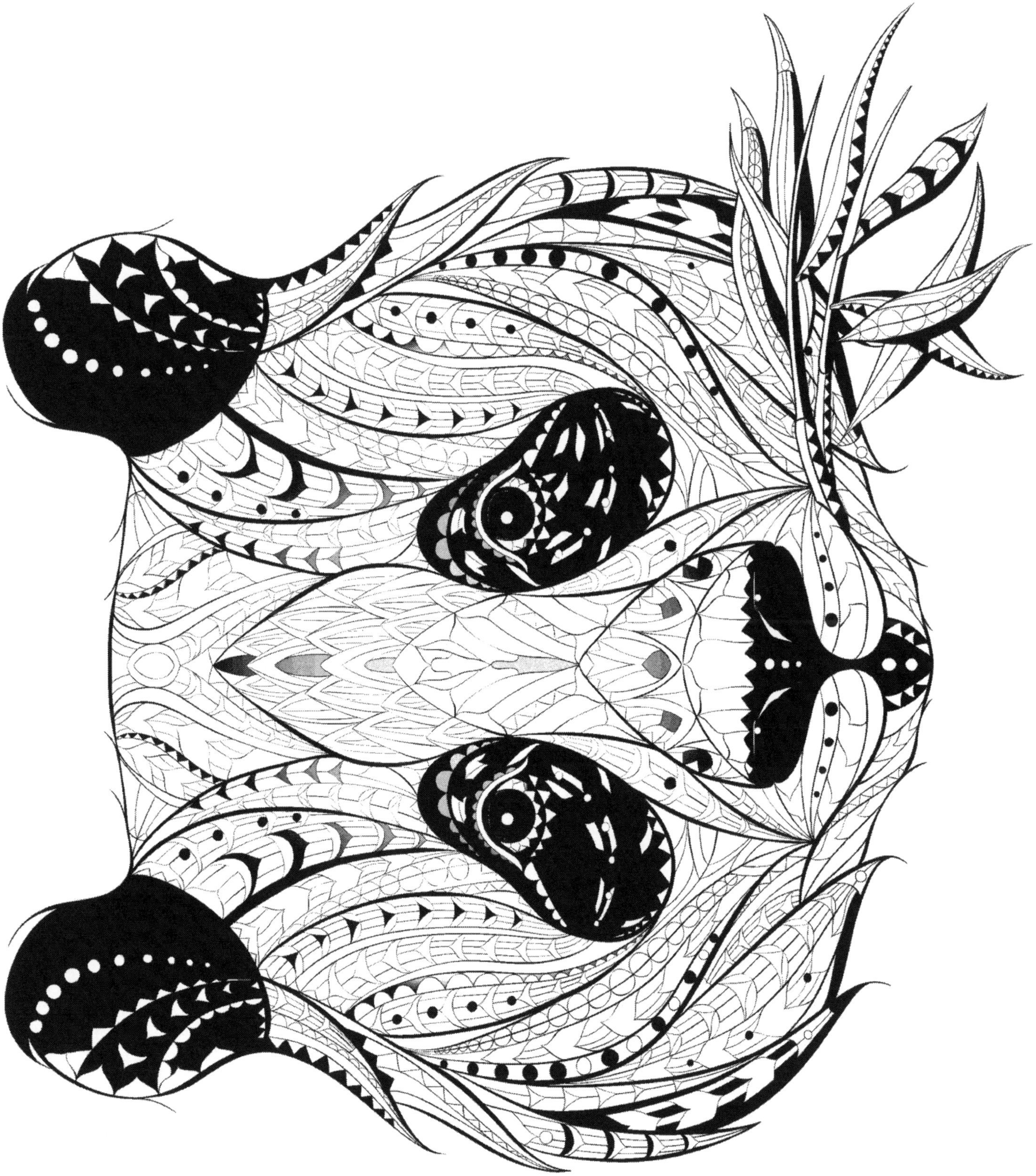

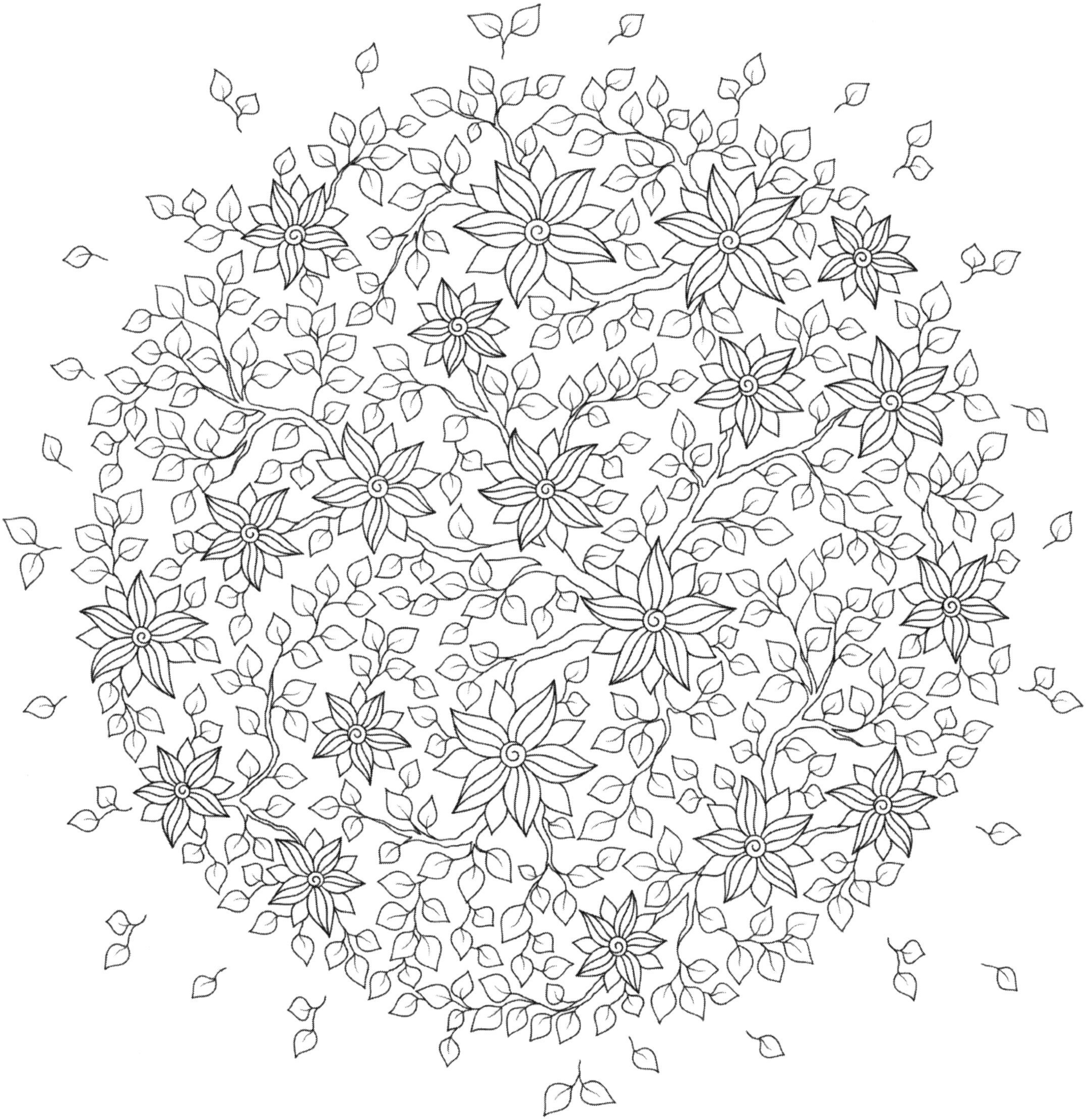

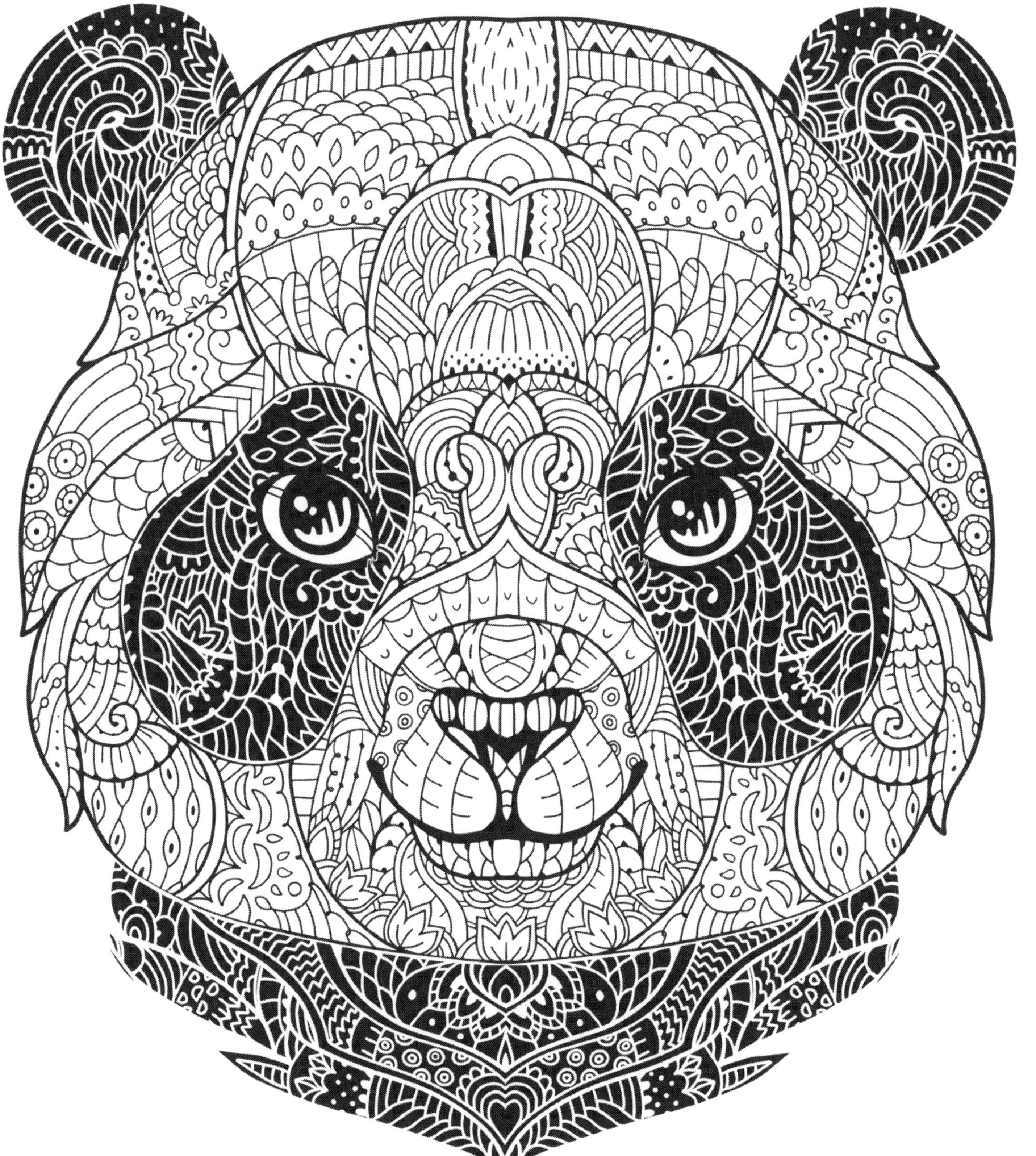

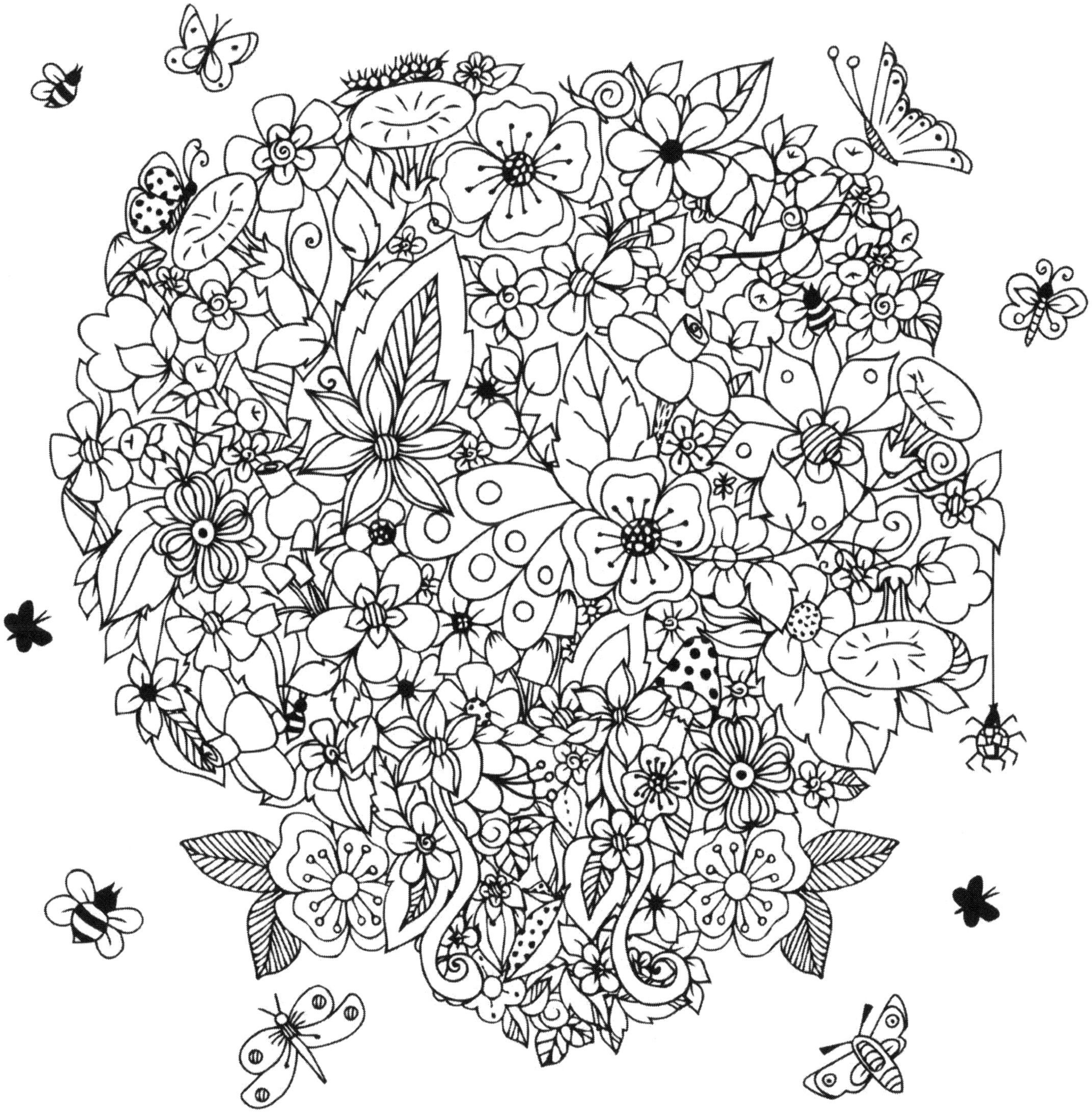

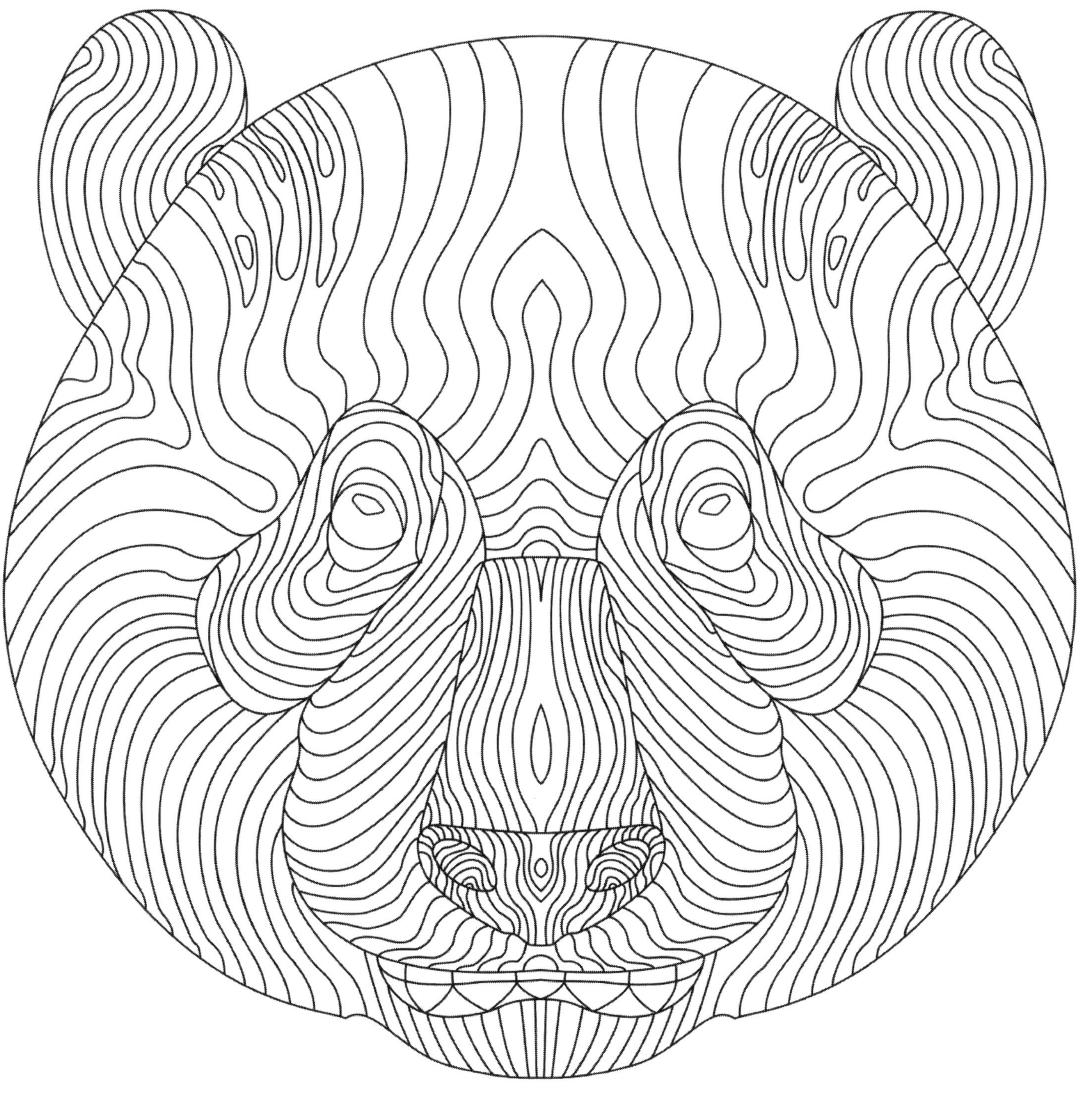

Download Free 15 Coloring Pages
http://eepurl.com/c0jb1r

Printed in Great Britain
by Amazon